X-TREME FACTS: ANCIENT HISTORY

THE MAYA CIVILIZATION

by Catherine C. Finan

Minneapolis, Minnesota

Credits:

Title page, 19 top, 20 bottom, 22 bottom, John_Walker/Shutterstock; 4 top, IndianSummer/Shutterstock; 4 bottom left, Augusto Ferrer-Dalmau Nieto/Creative Commons; 4 bottom right, atryk Kosmider/Shutterstock.com; 5 top, Dge/Creative Commons; 5 middle, Valentyn Volkov/Shutterstock; 5 bottom, Bequest of Leonard C. Hanna, Jr./Public Domain; 5 bottom left, 5 bottom right, 6 bottom left, 14 left, 19 top left, 27 top, Vlad G/Shutterstock.com; 6 top, Simon Dannhauer/Shutterstock; 6 bottom middle, 6 bottom right, 10 left, 10 bottom right, 11 top, 11 bottom left, 11 bottom middle, 12 left, 12 right, 13 top left, 13 bottom left, 14 bottom right, 16 bottom left, 17 bottom right, 19 top right, 19 bottom left, 20 bottom, 20 bottom right, 24 bottom left, 25 top right, Anton_Ivanov/Shutterstock.com; 7 top, Ervin Escobar/Creative Commons; 7 top right, Wolfgang Sauber/Creative Commons; 7 bottom, Ovedc/Creative Commons; 7 bottom left, 10 top middle, 18 bottom middle, 25 bottom left, 25 bottom right, Patryk Kosmider/Shutterstock.com; 7 bottom right, nikitich viktoriya/Shutterstock.com; 8 top, Joshua Davenport/Shutterstock; 8 top left, My Ocean Production/Shutterstock; 8 top middle, ArtFamily/Shutterstock; 8 bottom, Jihan Nafiaa Zahri/Shutterstock; 9 top, Bmamlin/Public Domain; 9 top left, 15 bottom left, Maria Giulia Tolotti/Creative Commons; 9 top right, 27 top left, 27 bottom left, 27 bottom middle right, Lucy.Brown/Shutterstock.com; 9 bottom, G Concha C/Creative Commons; 9 bottom left, unknown Maya artist/Public Domain; 9 bottom right, Tetris Awakening/Shutterstock; 15 top bottom, Drew McArthur/Shutterstock; 10 bottom left, Dotted Yeti/Shutterstock; 10 top middle, Wanchai Orsuk/Shutterstock; 10 top, Declan Hillman/Shutterstock; 10 bottom, Filip Fuxa/Shutterstock; 11 top right, Dalton Dingelstad/Shutterstock; 11 middle, Pixel-Shot/Shutterstock; 11 bottom, GTS Productions/Shutterstock; 11 bottom middle, 11 upper right, bottom, trabachar/Shutterstock; 11 bottom right, 24 bottom right, Jeka/Shutterstock; 12, Photo Spirit/Shutterstock; 12 bottom middle, Ziko van Dijk/Creative Commons; 13 top, LaiQuocAnh/Shutterstock; 13 top right, Leonard G./Public Domain; 13 bottom, soft_light/Shutterstock; 13 bottom right, Oleg Elkov/Shutterstock.com; 14 bottom, Ismamq/Creative Commons; 14 right, Public Domain; 15 top, 3dmotus/Shutterstock; 15 top left, Daderot/Creative Commons; 15 middle, Simon Burchell/Creative Commons; 15 bottom, Piotr Krzeslak/Shutterstock; 15 bottom middle, Gorodenkoff/Shutterstock; 15 bottom right, Roman Samborskyi/Shutterstock; 16 top, Public Domain; 16 bottom, John_Walker/Shutterstock; 16 bottom middle, veleknez/Shutterstock; 17 top, Jean Frédéric de Waldeck/Public Domain; 17 top right, Monica Romero A./Creative Commons; 17 bottom, K_Boonnitrod/Shutterstock; 17 bottom left, Pedro Lira Rencoret/Public Domain; 18 top, Vadim Petrakov/Shutterstock; 18 bottom, milosk50/Shutterstock; 18 bottom left and right, Design Projects/Shutterstock; 19 bottom middle, tandemich/Shutterstock; 19 bottom right, Michael C. Gray/Shutterstock; 21 to, ben bryant/Shutterstock; 21 bottom left, Michel wal/Creative Commons; 21 bottom right, Nutlegal Photographer/Shutterstock; 22 top, Tony Hisgett/Creative Commons; 22 bottom left, 22 bottom right, 23 bottom left, Sputnik/Creative Commons; 23 top, Gumr51/Creative Commons; 23 middle, Martin Bergsma/Shutterstock; 23 bottom, Iamnao/Shutterstock; 23 bottom right, Katiekk/Shutterstock.com; 24 middle, Sergey Nivens/Shutterstock; 24 middle top, SciePro/Shutterstock; 24 bottom, Tarcisio Schnaider/Shutterstock; 25 top, Gabriele Maltinti/Shutterstock; 25 top left, nortongo/Shutterstock; 25 bottom, Leonid Andronov/Shutterstock; 26 top, Bjørn Christian Tørrissen/Creative Commons; 26 top left, ImageArc/Shutterstock.com; 26 right, Watchara Samsuvan/Shutterstock; 27 bottom, fischers/Shutterstock; 27 bottom middle left, Sippman12's/Shutterstock; 27 bottom right, sashahaltam/Shutterstock; 28 top left, Aleksandar Todorovic/Shutterstock.com; 28 bottom left, Jose de Jesus Churion Del/Shutterstock.com; 28–29, Austen Photography

President: Jen Jenson
Director of Product Development: Spencer Brinker
Senior Editor: Allison Juda
Associate Editor: Charly Haley
Designer: Colin O'Dea

Developed and produced for Bearport Publishing by BlueAppleWorks Inc.
Managing Editor for BlueAppleWorks: Melissa McClellan
Art Director: T.J. Choleva
Photo Research: Jane Reid

Library of Congress Cataloging-in-Publication Data

Names: Finan, Catherine C., 1972- author.
Title: The Maya civilization / Catherine C. Finan.
Description: Minneapolis, Minnesota : Bearport Publishing, [2022] | Series: X-treme facts: ancient history | Includes bibliographical references and index.
Identifiers: LCCN 2021003691 (print) | LCCN 2021003692 (ebook) | ISBN 9781636910987 (library binding) | ISBN 9781636911052 (paperback) | ISBN 9781636911120 (ebook)
Subjects: LCSH: Mayas--History--Juvenile literature. | Mayas--Social life and customs--Juvenile literature. | Mexico--Civilization--Juvenile literature. | Central America--Civilization--Juvenile literature.
Classification: LCC F1435 .F57 2022 (print) | LCC F1435 (ebook) | DDC 972.81/016--dc23
LC record available at https://lccn.loc.gov/2021003691
LC ebook record available at https://lccn.loc.gov/2021003692

Copyright © 2022 Bearport Publishing Company. All rights reserved. No part of this publication may be reproduced in whole or in part, stored in any retrieval system, or transmitted in any form or by any means, electronic, mechanical, photocopying, recording, or otherwise, without written permission from the publisher.

For more information, write to Bearport Publishing, 5357 Penn Avenue South, Minneapolis, MN 55419.
Printed in the United States of America.

Contents

Meet the Maya 4
Step inside a City 6
Peer into the Pyramids 8
Religion Rules 10
Blood and Sacrifice 12
Meet the Gods 14
It Is Written 16
One Cool Calendar 18
Extreme Beauty 20
Play Ball! 22
Mystery of the Maya 24
The Maya Today 26

Mayan Weaving 28
Glossary 30
Read More 31
Learn More Online 31
Index 32
About the Author 32

Meet the Maya

Imagine wandering through a dense green jungle in Central America. You crawl under some branches and through some leaves . . . and suddenly you see a huge ancient stone pyramid! You've just discovered part of the magnificent Maya civilization! The ancient Maya lived throughout Mexico and Central America as early as 1,000 BCE. Their civilization reached its peak between 300 CE and 660 CE—and then it mysteriously disappeared!

The ancient Maya lived in Mexico's Yucatán Peninsula and in parts of today's Guatemala, Belize, El Salvador, and Honduras.

The name *Maya* came from the Spanish word for one of their cities, *Mayapán*.

Some Mayan cities may still be hidden in the jungle. The tallest pyramid in Mexico—in the ancient Mayan city of Tonina—wasn't discovered until 2010!

WHAT CAN I SAY? I AM VERY GOOD AT HIDE-AND-SEEK!

You can thank the Maya for chocolate. They made a drink from **cacao beans** for **rituals** and celebrations.

Cacao beans were so valuable, they were used as money. They were also used to make glue. What a waste of chocolate!

The Maya gathered honey from the stingless bees they raised.

CAN I HAVE SOME OF THAT HOT CHOCOLATE? I'LL TRADE YOU HONEY FOR IT!

SORRY, THIS IS ACTUALLY A POT OF CACAO GLUE.

Step inside a City

Unlike other ancient civilizations, Mayan cities didn't unite to form an **empire** under a single powerful leader. Though Mayan cities shared similar culture and religion, each city had its own ruler and government. Still, each city was designed in the same way. There was the king's palace and a central **plaza** where people traded for things.

The Maya built hundreds of cities. As many as 70,000 people lived in the Mayan city of Tikal, in today's Guatemala.

Some of Tikal's greatest rulers were women.

The palace of King Pakal in Palenque still stands in Mexico. King Pakal ruled for 68 years—longer than any other Mayan ruler!

THIS MASK ISN'T AS COMFORTABLE AS THEY SAID IT WOULD BE.

King Pakal became ruler at age 12. When he died, he was buried wearing a death mask made of green **jade**.

Mayan rulers were constantly at war with each other. That's not very neighborly!

Prisoners taken during wars between Mayan cities were **sacrificed** to the gods. Yikes!

WHY DO WE KEEP FIGHTING EACH OTHER?

IT'S NOTHING PERSONAL. WE JUST NEED MORE SACRIFICES.

Peer into the Pyramids

Mayan cities had amazing palaces and plazas—but even more impressive were their pyramids! The pyramids rose high above other buildings. They represented mountains, which people believed were linked to the gods' powers. One kind of pyramid had steep steps up the sides and a temple at the top, where priests performed sacrifices. Another kind was even steeper and considered more **sacred**. This kind of pyramid was completely off-limits to people.

El Castillo in Chichén Itzá has 365 steps—one for each day in a year!

Mayan pyramids were built to line up with the changing positions of the sun, stars, and planets.

During the spring and autumn **equinoxes**, the setting sun makes a shadow that looks like a serpent slithering down El Castillo's steps!

Religion Rules

As their pyramid temples show, ancient Mayan life revolved around religion, the gods, and the afterlife. The Maya believed the universe had three parts—Earth, sky, and the **underworld**. They thought a giant tree connected them, with roots in the underworld and branches high in the sky.

The Mayan view of death wasn't for the faint of heart. The afterlife was a journey from the underworld to the sky, complete with terrifying gods that scared the dead and sent them in the wrong direction!

The dead had to climb nine levels of the underworld to reach Earth and then thirteen more to reach the sky. What a workout!

Gods in the underworld had names like Flying Scab, Bloody Claws, and Pus Master. *Yuck!*

The underworld was also said to have **dead trees and rivers filled with blood and pus.**

The Temple of **Inscriptions** has nine levels, symbolizing the levels of the underworld.

To help the dead survive the underworld, they were buried with **tools, weapons, dogs . . . and hot chocolate!**

Blood and Sacrifice

While the Maya's view of death and the afterlife was pretty dark, their religious rituals were outright bloody. The Maya believed they could communicate with the gods by shedding their blood. They pierced their own flesh, and priests even offered up human sacrifices. If bloody rituals aren't your thing, just turn the page . . .

People who were sacrificed to the gods often had their hearts cut out and placed on statues.

Being sacrificed to the gods was considered a great honor.

CONGRATULATIONS! YOU'RE THE LUCKY ONES WE CHOSE!

I DON'T FEEL VERY LUCKY!

I RESPECTFULLY DECLINE THIS HONOR. I'M OUT OF HERE!

Sacrifice victims were often offered to the rain god, Chac, and painted blue in his honor.

At first, only nobles and other high-ranking Maya were offered as sacrifices. Their blood was thought to be purer.

The Maya pierced their tongues, lips, and ears with stingray spines. Sometimes thorns were pulled through the piercings, too. *Ouch!*

Cheer up! People who were sacrificed skipped the scary afterlife journey and went straight to the sky.

Meet the Gods

Human sacrifice sounds a bit harsh today, but for the ancient Maya, it was all about keeping the gods happy. If the gods were unhappy, the people would pay! The Maya believed their gods controlled everything from the weather to the **harvest**. One of the most important gods was Itzamna, the god of fire. People believed he helped create Earth and controlled day and night. Itzamna and his fellow gods were a busy bunch!

Each city had a special god who was invited to live in its main temple and bring blessings to the city!

Itzamna ruled over the sky and gave the Maya their calendar, writing system, art, and medicine. Talk about an overachiever!

People believed that the Mayan god Chac struck the clouds with his lightning ax to make rain. Cool trick!

A Mayan jaguar god symbolized the nighttime sun, journeying through the underworld until the sun rose again.

It Is Written

Ancient Mayan priests didn't spend all their time offering sacrifices to the gods. They were also among the only Maya who learned to write. The Mayan writing system used symbols to represent different objects, words, or sounds. The priests wrote stories on paper made from tree bark that was folded together in leather and bound to make a book called a codex. A few of these books are still around today.

The Dresden Codex is the oldest piece of ancient Mayan writing, dating to almost 900 years ago. It tells the story of a great flood.

The Maya wrote with turkey feathers dipped in ink made from coal.

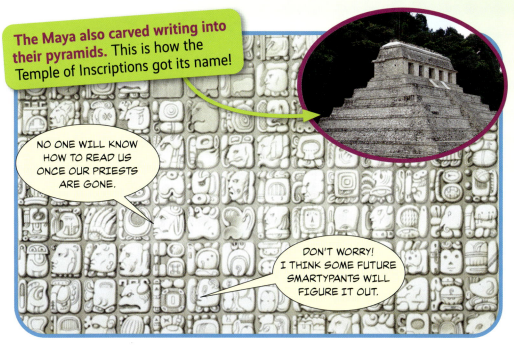

The Maya also carved writing into their pyramids. This is how the Temple of Inscriptions got its name!

NO ONE WILL KNOW HOW TO READ US ONCE OUR PRIESTS ARE GONE.

DON'T WORRY! I THINK SOME FUTURE SMARTYPANTS WILL FIGURE IT OUT.

The Mayan writing system had more than 1,000 symbols, but only about 300 to 500 were used at any time.

Spanish people discovered Mayan books in the 1500s, but they burned them, believing they were evil.

The few surviving Mayan books focus on rituals, **astronomy**, and the Mayan calendar!

WE'VE GOT A FIRE ALL SET UP. WHERE ARE YOUR BOOKS?

I GUESS YOU MUST NOT BE A BIG READER.

One Cool Calendar

Mayan priests also studied math and astronomy. The priests used this knowledge to create a highly accurate calendar. Actually, they created three different calendars that worked together! A sacred calendar charted the planets and stars, and predicted future events. A solar calendar tracked the days and seasons. And a Long Count calendar recorded Mayan history!

The first Mayan calendars were carved in stone almost 2,500 years ago!

The Maya believed Earth was created on August 11, 3114 BCE.

The Mayan solar calendar had 18 months with 20 days each, as well as an extra 5-day month. This added up to 365 days—just like modern calendars!

The five extra days of the Mayan calendar were called Wayeb. They were considered very unlucky.

Every 52 years, the sacred and solar calendars began on the same day. On this day, the Maya held a New Fire Festival to celebrate new beginnings.

People thought the ancient Mayan calendars showed the end of the world on December 21, 2012—but it turns out they had been reading the calendars wrong!

Extreme Beauty

The priests and kings were at the top of Mayan society. Life was much easier for them than it was for **commoners**, who worked long hours farming and making tools. While the king, priests, and nobles lived in palaces, commoners lived in one-room huts. Wealthy people wore colorful clothes and **headdresses**, while poorer people wore simpler clothing. But across all ranks of society, the things people did to make themselves pretty were . . . pretty *interesting*!

The ancient Maya often wore headdresses. **The more important you were, the bigger your headdress!**

HOW DO YOU KEEP YOUR HEAD UP WITH THAT THING ON?

HOW CAN YOU STAND TO BE SO UNIMPORTANT?

The Maya pierced, tattooed, and **shaped their bodies** for beauty and to please the gods.

Large noses were considered beautiful to the Maya. They would use makeup to make their noses look larger.

TRUE! BUT YOUR TATTOOS ARE SIMPLY FABULOUS!

I CAN'T EVEN LOOK AT YOU! YOUR NOSE IS SO MUCH BIGGER THAN MINE!

Both men and women were tattooed after marriage. Men even tattooed their faces.

The Maya's idea of beauty included a long, flat forehead. Some even wrapped their children's heads tightly to change the shape of their skulls!

The Maya filed their teeth, drilled holes in them, and filled them with colorful stones such as jade and **turquoise**.

CHECK OUT MY PERFECTLY FLAT MAYAN HEAD!

THAT'S NOTHING. YOU SHOULD SEE MY SMILE!

Play Ball!

Whether you were a Mayan king or commoner, you were probably a big fan of ball games. But these weren't like today's games of baseball or football—they were much more difficult! In the Mayan ball game, two teams competed to put a large rubberlike ball through a stone ring without using their hands or feet. And if that weren't hard enough, some players may have even been sacrificed.

A large ball court is still standing at Chichén Itzá. A player's whisper at one end of the court could be heard at the other.

Players could only touch the ball with their hips, knees, shoulders, or elbows.

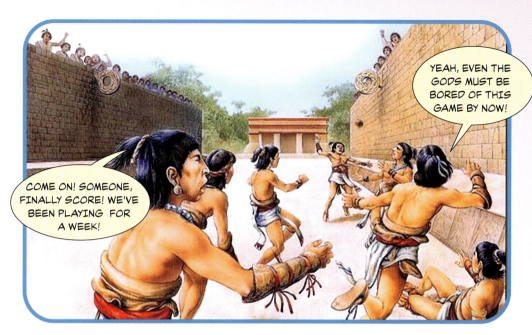

Ball games were played to please the gods. Scoring a point was so difficult that a game could go on for days!

The soccer-sized balls were covered by a substance also used to make chewing gum. They may have had human skulls inside them!

The Maya believed that playing the ball game more often would bring a better harvest.

Mystery of the Maya

The Maya's ball courts still stand, as do many of their pyramids and palaces. But what happened to their mighty civilization? Though the arrival of Spanish colonists in the 1500s violently changed the region forever, they were not responsible for the Maya's disappearance. The Maya civilization reached its peak between the years 300 and 660, but then it quickly declined by 900—and no one really knows why! Of course, there are some theories . . .

At its peak, the Maya civilization had about 2,000 people for every 1 square mile (2.6 sq km). That's similar to Los Angeles today!

Mayan cities often warred with one another. Did so much fighting finally lead to the civilization's fall?

By the year 950, there was only about 5 percent of the Maya population left.

The Maya Today

Although the civilization mysteriously disappeared, the people did not. Today, about six million Maya live in Mexico and Central America. Many of them still speak the Mayan language. The days of blood sacrifices at temple pyramids are long gone, but the modern Maya still hold some **traditional** Mayan beliefs. Their culture continues to influence the world today, with a legacy that can be felt around the globe.

Ceremonies such as a winter solstice celebration are still held at Tikal.

WHY IS THERE A BONFIRE DOWN BELOW, AND WHY ARE WE HOLDING CANDLES?

TO CELEBRATE THE RETURN OF LIGHT IN THE DARKNESS OF WINTER!

The Maya invented an early version of rubber using sap from rubber trees.

The Maya came up with the idea of the number zero more than 2,000 years ago.

About 80 percent of the ancient Maya's language is still spoken today.

Cultural **reenactments** help today's Maya preserve and share their heritage.

The Maya may have been the first people to raise turkeys for food. They also used turkey feathers and bones to make tools and instruments.

A Mayan legend says a peasant invented the corn tortilla 12,000 years ago as a gift to a king!

Mayan Weaving
Craft Project

The Mayan Moon goddess Ix Chel was believed to have taught the first woman how to weave. Since then, the Maya have spun plant fibers into thread. The threads are then dyed and woven into fabrics that are bursting with color. Try your hand at a Mayan-style weaving!

The Maya are very proud of their unique weaving patterns and traditions.

Weaving colorful, handmade fabrics takes many hours of work.

What You Will Need

- Scissors
- A round, plastic container lid
- Yarn
- Tape

Step One

Using scissors, carefully cut nine evenly spaced notches around the edge of the plastic lid.

Step Two

Cut a piece of yarn about 24 inches (60 cm) long. Tape one end to the center of the top of the lid.

Step Three

Turn the lid over and pull the yarn through one notch and into a notch at the opposite side. Then, pull the yarn into the notch just to the right of the first one you put the yarn through. Next, pull it through the notch directly opposite, making an X shape. Repeat this process until you pull the yarn through the ninth notch.

Step Four

Bring the yarn to the center of your lid and start to weave over and under the yarn lines you have created, moving to the right in a circular direction from the center of the lid toward the outer edge.

Step Five

When you reach the end of your yarn, tie a new color of yarn to the one you were weaving with. Keep weaving until the lid is covered. Tuck the end of the last piece of yarn under the other yarn and tape it in place. Beautiful!

astronomy the study of objects beyond Earth, such as the sun, moon, stars, and planets

cacao beans the dried seeds of a tropical tree that are used to make cocoa and chocolate

commoners people of low rank in society

empire a group of countries or regions ruled by a single person

equinoxes the two days in the year (the first days of spring and autumn) when day and night are the same length

harvest the picking or gathering of food crops that are ready to be eaten

headdresses coverings or decorations for the head

inscriptions words cut into a surface

jade a hard green stone used in jewelry

plaza a public square or open space in the middle of a town or city

reenactments actions or events of the past that are performed or acted out in modern times to help teach history and culture

rituals special ceremonies for religious or other purposes

sacred very holy; deserving great respect and honor

sacrificed killed or offered as an act of worship to a god

traditional a way of thinking, behaving, or doing something that a group of people have done for many years

turquoise a blue or bluish-green mineral used in jewelry

underworld a place where the ancient Maya believed dead people and spirits live

Read More

Green, Sara. *Ancient Maya (Blastoff! Discovery: Ancient Civilizations).* Minneapolis: Bellwether Media, 2020.

Green, Sara. *Chichén Itzá (Blastoff! Discovery: The Seven Wonders of the Modern World).* Minneapolis: Bellwether Media, 2021.

Williams, Brian. *Maya, Incas, and Aztecs (DK Findout!).* New York: DK Publishing, 2018.

Learn More Online

1. Go to **www.factsurfer.com**
2. Enter "**Maya Civilization**" into the search box.
3. Click on the cover of this book to see a list of websites.

Index

afterlife 10, 12–13
astronomy 17–18
ball game 22–23
blood 10, 12–13, 26
calendar 14, 17–19
Chac 13, 15
Chichén Itzá 8, 22
chocolate 5, 11
codex 16
El Castillo 8–9
gods 7–10, 12–16, 20, 23, 28
Itzamna 9, 14

King Pakal 7
Kukulkan 9, 15
Mexico 4–5, 7, 9, 26
Palenque 7
priests 8, 12, 16–18, 20
pyramids 4–5, 8–10, 17, 24, 26
sacrifices 7–8, 12–14, 16, 23, 26
Spanish 4, 17, 24
Temple of Inscriptions 11, 17
underworld 10–11, 15
writing 14, 16–17

About the Author

Catherine C. Finan is a writer living in northeastern Pennsylvania. She enjoys writing about a wide range of subjects, including ancient history. She once climbed a Mayan pyramid in Cobá, Mexico.